ASTRONOMY, ASTRONAUTS and SPACE EXPLORATION

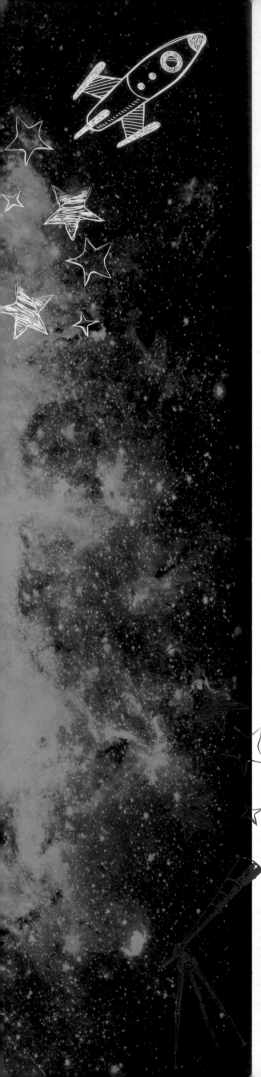

Published in paperback in 2016
First published in hardback in 2015
© Wayland 2015

Wayland
An imprint of
Hachette Children's Group
Part of Hodder & Stoughton
Carmelite House
50 Victoria Embankment
London EC4Y 0DZ

Produced by White-Thomson Publishing Ltd.

White-Thomson Publishing Ltd
www.wtpub.co.uk
+44 (0) 843 208 7460

Editor: Izzi Howell
Designer: Clare Nicholas
Cover design and concept: Lisa Peacock

A catalogue for this title is available from the British Library

ISBN: 978 0 7502 9230 6

Library eBook ISBN: 978 0 7502 9229 0

Dewey Number: 520-dc23

10 9 8 7 6 5 4 3 2 1

Printed in China

MIX
Paper from
responsible sources
FSC
www.fsc.org
FSC® C104740

Wayland is a division of Hachette Children's Books,
an Hachette UK company.

www.hachette.co.uk

The website addresses (URLs) included in this book were valid at the time of going to press. However, because of the nature of the Internet, it is possible that some addresses may have changed, or sites may have changed or closed down since publication. While the author and publisher regret any inconvenience this may cause the readers, no responsibility for any such changes can be accepted by either the author or the publisher.

Picture credits
Shutterstock/nienora cover (background), Shutterstock/Vadim Sadovski cover (tl), Shutterstock/notkoo cover (tl), Shutterstock/Antony McAulay cover (c), Shutterstock/godrick cover (bl), Shutterstock/Petrafler cover (bl), Shutterstock/Fer Gregory cover (br), Shutterstock/A-R-T title page (background), NASA title page (centre).

Thinkstock/hugocorzo 4 (bl), Shutterstock/oorka 4 (br), Shutterstock/Asmus 5 (tr), Shutterstock/andromina 5 (bl), Shutterstock/Tribalium 5 (br), Justus Sustermans/Wikimedia 6 (tr), Kerry Flaherty and Q2A Solutions 6 (br), English School, [c.1715-1720]/Wikimedia 7 (tr), Kerry Flaherty and Q2A Solutions 7 (cl), Shutterstock/Bryan Solomon 7 (br), Gordon Chesterman - www.gcmediatenerife.com 8 (bl), Shutterstock/Kapreski 8 (br), NASA/Jim Ross 9, Kerry Flaherty and Q2A Solutions 10, NASA/Goddard/SDO AIA Team 11 (tr), NASA/JPL-Caltech and The Hubble Heritage Team (STScI/AURA) 11 (br), Shutterstock/Manamana 12 (l), NRAO/AUI/NSF 12 (r), National Science Foundation 13 (cl), Shutterstock/RedKoala 13 (cr), Shutterstock/Fenton one 13 (bl), NASA 14 (bl), Raghvendra Sahai and John Trauger (JPL)/the WFPC2 science team/NASA 14 (br), NASA/Ball Aerospace 15 (tr), Shutterstock/RedKoala 15 (bl), NASA 16, NASA 17 (tr), Shutterstock/Alhovik 17 (cl), Shutterstock/andromina 17 (br), NASA/JPL-Caltech/UCLA/McREL 18 (tr), Shutterstock/PrOlena 18 (bl), ESA 19 (tr), NASA/LEGO 19 (bl), Shutterstock/Mickicev Atelje 19 (br), NASA/JPL-Caltech/UMD 20, NASA/JPL-Caltech 21 (c), Shutterstock/WonderfulPixel 21 (bl), NASA 22 (tr), Shutterstock/bioraven 22 (bl) NASA 23 (c), Shutterstock/joingate 23 (br), NASA 24, Shutterstock/bioraven 25 (tr), NASA 25 (bc), NASA 26, NASA 27 (tr), Shutterstock/Swill Klitch 27 (bl), Shutterstock/andromina 27 (br), NASA 28 (bl), Shutterstock/RedKoala 28 (br), NASA 29.

Design elements throughout: Shutterstock/PinkPueblo, Shutterstock/topform, Shutterstock/Nikiteev_Konstantin, Shutterstock/Vadim Sadovski, Shutterstock/Shutterstock/Elinalee, Shutterstock/mhatzapa, Shutterstock/notkoo, Shutterstock/Hilch.

CONTENTS

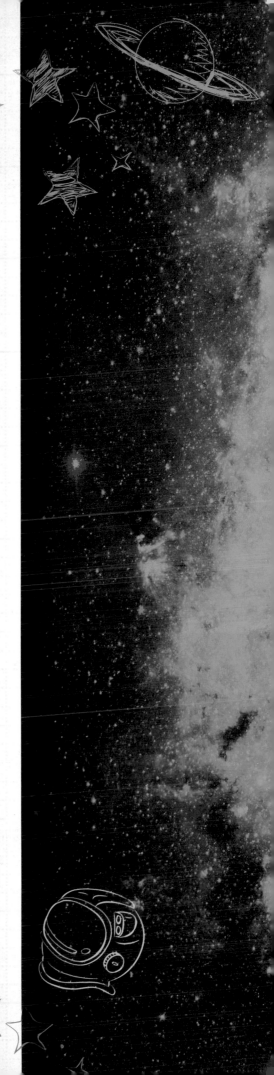

STARGAZING

Ancient peoples have always looked up and marvelled at the night sky. Some went further, studying the movement of stars and planets to help them navigate or build accurate calendars. Over time, the investigation of space became the science of astronomy.

Tracking Movement

Changes in the patterns of stars, caused by Earth's orbit of the Sun, were used by past civilisations to predict the seasons. The ancient Egyptians used the position of the star Sirius, which they called the Star of Isis, as a guide to when the Nile River would flood farmland each year.

ANCIENT BELIEFS

The ancient Egyptians thought that the Sun was a god, Ra, who was swallowed every evening by a night-sky goddess called Nut. The ancient Chinese were fearful of solar eclipses, as they believed that a giant dragon had eaten the Sun.

WHO WERE HO AND HSI?

According to legend, Ho and Hsi were ancient Chinese astronomers, responsible for predicting when solar eclipses would occur. When they failed to predict the eclipse in 2136 BCE, the Chinese emperor had them executed!

solar eclipse

This Mayan observatory was built around 906 CE. Mayan astronomers were able to predict the length of Venus's orbit of the Sun to within two hours without telescopes.

Great Greeks

The ancient Greeks made many important discoveries, from Aristarchus figuring out that Earth spins on its own axis, to Thales predicting a solar eclipse. The ancient Greeks also gave us the term planet, from *planētēs*, meaning wanderer. This was inspired by the planets' movement across the night sky.

AMAZING BRAHE

Tycho Brahe was a 16th-century Danish nobleman who was fascinated by astronomy. Over years of observation, he built up an incredibly accurate catalogue of over 960 stars – all spotted with the naked eye, as telescopes had not yet been invented. Brahe's assistant, Johannes Kepler, would go on to prove that planets orbit the Sun in an oval path.

This is a statue of Tycho Brahe in Copenhagen, Denmark.

36

THE NUMBER OF STARS DETAILED IN THE OLDEST KNOWN STAR CATALOGUE, CALLED *THREE STARS EACH*. IT WAS WRITTEN ON CLAY TABLETS BY THE ANCIENT BABYLONIANS MORE THAN 3,200 YEARS AGO.

Tycho Brahe lost much of his nose in a duelling accident, but made himself a false nose out of metal and wax!

OPTICAL TELESCOPES

The first telescopes were invented around 1608 by Dutch spectacle makers, who placed glass lenses in a tube to magnify objects. Many early telescopes were used by merchants and sailors to spot distant ships.

Looking Up

The Italian scientist Galileo Galilei did not invent the first telescope, but he was one of the first to point it skywards. He detected sunspots on the Sun's surface and was the first person to see Jupiter's four largest moons: Io, Callisto, Ganymede and Europa.

Galileo Galilei

REFRACTING TELESCOPES

Galileo's telescope was a refractor, gathering in light through an aperture of 1.5 cm – around twice the size of your pupil. The bigger the aperture, the greater the amount of light that can be gathered in. When people started building telescopes with bigger apertures and lenses, they could see distant objects in greater detail.

Refracting telescope

4. Eyepiece lens magnifies the image.

1. Light travels through the aperture.

3. Light meets at the focal point.

2. Objective lens bends (refracts) light, focusing it.

Mirror, Mirror

In 1668, Sir Isaac Newton was the first person to make a reflecting telescope, by replacing lenses with mirrors. It proved to be a practical design as it didn't need a huge aperture to see distant objects. Mirrors also weigh less than lenses, suffer less distortion and are easier to make at large sizes.

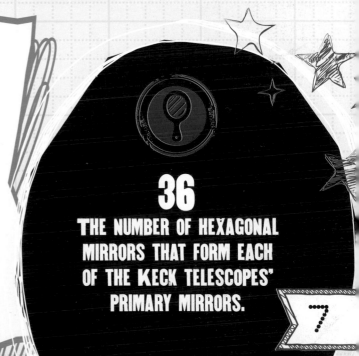

Sir Isaac Newton

Reflecting telescope

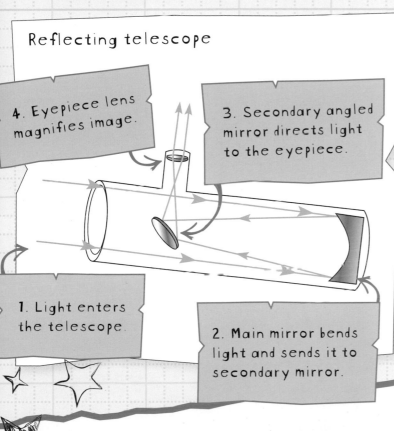

4. Eyepiece lens magnifies image.

3. Secondary angled mirror directs light to the eyepiece.

1. Light enters the telescope.

2. Main mirror bends light and sends it to secondary mirror.

HOW BIG IS THE LARGEST REFLECTING TELESCOPE?

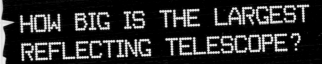

The current largest reflecting telescope is the Gran Telescopio Canarias, with a mirror diameter of 10.4 m. However, telescopes with mirrors up to 40 m in diameter will be ready within the next ten years.

TELESCOPES TODAY

The giant 10-m aperture and mirror of the Keck I telescope allow it to peer deep into space. But when linked to its twin, Keck II, the pair of telescopes can see even further. In 1999, the Keck telescopes were the first optical telescopes to view an exoplanet and spot stars swirling round the giant black hole at the centre of the Milky Way galaxy.

36
THE NUMBER OF HEXAGONAL MIRRORS THAT FORM EACH OF THE KECK TELESCOPES' PRIMARY MIRRORS.

OBSERVATORIES

Large telescopes are often housed with computers and specialist cameras in observatories. These are built in remote locations, away from cities whose lights could interfere with observations, and in dry places with few clouds to get in the way.

Remote Controlled

Observatories typically house their telescopes in protective domes, which can open up when viewing is required. Computers control the telescope's precise positioning. Some, like the Bradford Robotic Telescope, can be controlled via a computer network so that instructions can be sent from anywhere in the world.

SHAPING UP

The air in the atmosphere above a telescope is constantly moving, which can blur images. Some scientific telescopes compensate for this by using adaptive optics. This technology consists of a computer and additional mirror that can change shape according to the air movement, helping to sharpen up the telescope's images.

The Bradford Robotic Telescope pictured under the Milky Way.

26

THE NUMBER OF DIFFERENT TELESCOPES HOUSED AT THE KITT PEAK NATIONAL OBSERVATORY IN ARIZONA – THE LARGEST GROUPING OF ASTRONOMICAL INSTRUMENTS IN THE WORLD.

Splitting Light

Apart from telescopes, observatories feature other instruments including photometers, which measure how bright an object is, and spectrographs, which divide up light coming from a star or another object, into different colours called a spectrum. Astronomers can analyse spectrums to learn what gases an object is made from.

HOW OLD IS THE OLDEST OBSERVATORY?

Many ancient peoples built places to observe the stars and planets. The oldest of these observatories is the Goseck Circle, in Germany. Used to map the Sun's path, it is over 6,800 years old!

TAKE-OFF TELESCOPE

A modified Boeing 747 has been turned into a flying observatory that can travel above Earth's atmosphere to obtain a clearer view of space. Called SOFIA, the US–German observatory has a 2.5-m reflecting telescope and instruments to study the infrared waves given off by newborn and dying stars.

SOFIA flying over the Sierra Nevada mountains, USA.

SOFIA's telescope door is open while in flight.

SEEING OTHER WAVES

Gamma rays, X-rays and radio waves are all types of electromagnetic radiation. Although invisible to our eyes, they can be collected and studied by astronomers using special instruments.

The Electromagnetic Spectrum

Each type of electromagnetic radiation, from radio waves to gamma rays, has its own wavelength – the distance between a point on one wave and the same point on the next wave. The shorter the wavelength, the greater the energy produced by the radiation. These wavelengths can be plotted on an electromagnetic spectrum.

wavelength

visible light

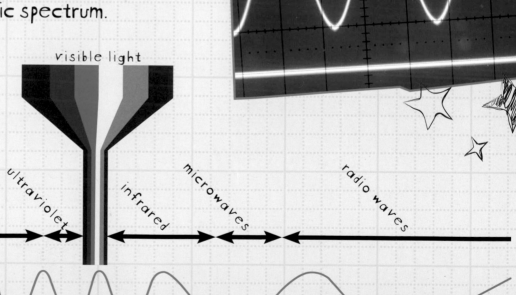

gamma rays   X-rays   ultraviolet   infrared   microwaves   radio waves

wavelength

energy

X-RAYS

Very hot stars, with temperatures of 1 million °C or higher, give off large amounts of X-rays. Exploding stars also produce X-rays, and so X-ray tracking instruments can record giant star explosions.

an ultraviolet image of the Sun

ULTRAVIOLET

Ultraviolet waves are shorter and have more energy than visible light. Many of the hottest stars in the universe give out most of their energy in the ultraviolet range.

GAMMA RAYS

Gamma rays have the shortest wavelength of all electromagnetic waves. They are released by the most energetic actions occurring in the universe, such as matter falling into a black hole. Most gamma rays are absorbed by Earth's atmosphere, so gamma-ray telescopes are either sent into space or carried high above Earth in high-altitude balloons.

INFRARED

Cooler objects, such as comets, give off infrared radiation. This has less energy than visible light, but can be spotted and measured using infrared telescopes.

an infrared image of the Sombrero Galaxy

RADIO ASTRONOMY

Radio waves have the longest wavelengths of all types of electromagnetic radiation. They travel through Earth's atmosphere and can be tracked by radio telescopes on the ground.

DIY Discoveries

Between 1937 and the mid-1940s, Grote Reber was the world's only radio astronomer! He built the first radio dish out of sheet metal and parts from an old Model T Ford truck, next to his mother's house in Chicago. Using his 9.75-m-wide dish, Reber made the first radio survey of space, discovering radio waves coming from many galaxies.

SEEING THE INVISIBLE

Many radio waves come from the cool gas found between stars that cannot be seen by optical telescopes. Radio waves travel through dust, so radio astronomy is incredibly useful for studying dusty areas of space, such as stellar nebulae or the centres of some galaxies.

On the right, the first radio dish, and on the left, the Very Large Array (VLA), a modern radio astronomy observatory made up of 27 radio antennas.

WHAT HAVE WE DISCOVERED THROUGH RADIO ASTRONOMY?

Radio astronomy has led to many discoveries, including a type of dense, fast-spinning star called a pulsar. Radio telescopes have also detected giant jets of gas shooting out from distant galaxies. The jet shooting from the centre of the M87 galaxy is thought to be 5,000 light years long!

Dishing It Up

Radio waves from space are usually gathered in by large, concave radio antenna dishes. The signals are increased in strength and then measured. To gather more radio waves, bigger dishes can be built or a series of small to medium-sized dishes can all work together, grouped in what astronomers call an array.

HEY, HEY, IT'S AN ARRAY!

The Square Kilometre Array (SKA) will be the world's biggest radio telescope when completed in the 2020s. It will feature thousands of small antennas working together, mostly in Australia and South Africa, to create a combined collecting area of about one square kilometre – a million square metres.

305

THE DIAMETER IN METRES OF THE LARGEST SINGLE RADIO TELESCOPE DISH, FOUND AT THE ARECIBO OBSERVATORY IN PUERTO RICO. THE DISH IS MADE UP OF OVER 38,000 ALUMINIUM PANELS JOINED TOGETHER.

the radio telescope dish at the Arecibo Observatory

Huge amounts of computing power will be needed to process signals from the SKA's antennas. The array's main computer will have as much power as 100 million personal computers!

OBSERVATORIES IN SPACE

Earth's atmosphere can distort visible light coming from space and block out other electromagnetic waves, such as gamma rays. So, telescopes and scientific instruments have been launched high above the atmosphere where they can observe space 24 hours a day.

The Hubble Space Telescope

The most famous space observatory of all is the 15.9-metre-long, 11-tonne Hubble Space Telescope. Launched in 1990, it orbits 559 km above Earth's surface. The instruments on board the Hubble can view ultraviolet, infrared and visible light, and are specially designed to require very little electricity. The Hubble operates on only 2,800 watts of power – about the same as an electric kettle.

SNAP HAPPY

The Hubble's powerful cameras have taken some of the most spectacular images ever seen of distant objects in space. Each week, the Hubble transmits around 120 gigabytes of images and data back to its command centre on Earth. By 2014, it had taken over 750,000 images of stars, galaxies and other bodies.

The Hubble Telescope captured this stunning hourglass pattern around a dying star.

The Hubble Telescope orbits Earth.

Hot and Cold

Launched in 1999, the Chandra Observatory gathers in X-rays given off by incredibly hot objects in space, such as the remains of exploding stars. In contrast, the Spitzer Observatory investigates cooler objects in space that give off infrared energy. Since its launch in 2003, Spitzer has spotted and tracked new comets, and discovered the largest, faintest ring around Saturn.

Scientists assemble parts of the Spitzer Observatory.

550
THE DISTANCE IN KILOMETRES FROM WHICH THE JWST WOULD BE ABLE TO SPOT A FOOTBALL-SIZED OBJECT. IT IS APPROXIMATELY SEVEN TIMES MORE POWERFUL THAN THE HUBBLE.

FOLD-OUT OBSERVATORY
The James Webb Space Telescope (JWST) is the Hubble's successor, with its launch planned for 2018. Both the observatory's 6.5-m mirror and its 18-m by 12.2-m protective sun shield (bigger than a tennis court!) are far too big to fit inside a rocket. They have been designed to fold up for launch, and then automatically fold out once the observatory is in space.

LIFT OFF!

Getting machines past Earth's gravity and into space takes a HUGE amount of power. There's only one type of engine capable of generating enough thrust to counteract the force of gravity and launch spacecraft into space – a rocket engine.

Action-Reaction

Rocket engines work on the principle that for every action there is an equal and opposite reaction. When a rocket engine burns fuel in a combustion chamber, it generates gases that blast out of the engine's exhaust (the action), forcing the rocket to travel in the opposite direction (the reaction).

SOLID OR LIQUID

There's no oxygen-rich air in space for fuel to burn in, so rockets have to carry their own oxygen or oxygen-creating chemicals, known as oxidisers, with them. These are mixed with the fuel and then burned. The Saturn V rocket burns over 15,000 kg of fuel and oxidiser each second when lifting off – more than the weight of two adult elephants.

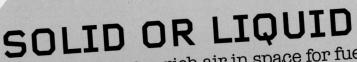

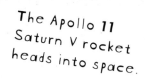

The Apollo 11 Saturn V rocket heads into space.

Getting A Boost

Some launch vehicles gain extra power from external rocket engines called boosters. These fire at launch and fall away minutes later, after exhausting all of their fuel. The two boosters used to launch the Space Shuttles generated enough energy in their first two minutes of firing to heat 87,000 homes for a day.

The Space Shuttle Challenger launches for the first time.

PAYLOADS

Rocket engines power a launch vehicle that contains the object to be carried into space, known as the payload. This may be a space probe or a manned spacecraft. The first living payload in space was a small collection of fruit flies sent into space in a V2 rocket in 1947.

WHAT IS THE BIGGEST EVER LAUNCH VEHICLE?

NASA's Saturn V rocket was 10.6 m wide and 110 m tall — taller than the Statue of Liberty. Its engines produced approximately 3.4 million kg of thrust at lift-off.

133

THE NUMBER OF SUCCESSFUL MISSIONS MADE BY NASA'S SPACE SHUTTLE REUSABLE LAUNCH VEHICLES. SPACE SHUTTLES BLASTED UP INTO SPACE USING ROCKET ENGINES, AND GLIDED BACK DOWN TO EARTH CARRYING UP TO SEVEN CREW MEMBERS.

SPACE PROBES

Space probes are machines sent on a one-way mission to explore space; most probes never return to Earth. Probes don't need lots of equipment, supplies or life-support systems, as they don't carry any passengers. They only need a power source, so they can be built smaller and cheaper than human-carrying spacecraft.

Super Solar

Space probes are powered by solar panels or by generators that use radioactive elements as fuel. Probes send back data, digital images and measurements to Earth via radio waves.

an artist's impression of DAWN orbiting the asteroid Vesta

FLY-BY

Many probes are designed to fly past planets, moons, asteroids or comets, taking measurements as they travel. Voyager 2 performed fly-bys of all four outer planets, whereas the DAWN probe performed a fly-by of Mars before orbiting the large asteroid Vesta and visiting the dwarf planet Ceres.

In 2011, the Lunar Reconnaissance Orbiter (LRO) space probe sent back 192 terabytes of photos and other information as it orbited the Moon — enough to fill 41,000 DVDs.

WHAT'S THE FURTHEST A SPACE PROBE HAS EXPLORED?

The Voyager 1 space probe was launched in 1977 and is still travelling. It is now over 19 billion km from Earth.

Locked In Orbit

Some space probes are sent to a planet or moon and go into orbit around it so they can study and photograph it. The Mars Express probe has been travelling around Mars since 2003, sending back huge amounts of information about the planet's atmosphere and surface. It has even performed a cheeky fly-by of Phobos, one of Mars's two moons.

an artist's impression of Philae on the surface of Comet 67P/C-G

LONG-TERM RELATIONSHIP

In 2014, after a ten-year, 6.4-billion-km journey, the Rosetta space probe finally got to within 100 km of its target, Comet 67P/C-G. Rosetta dropped a small probe called Philae onto the comet's nucleus, which bounced several times before landing. It sent back lots of data to scientists on Earth.

From right to left — the Roman god Jupiter, his wife Juno and the astronomer Galileo.

3

THE NUMBER OF ALUMINIUM LEGO FIGURES CARRIED ON BOARD THE JUNO SPACE PROBE, AS PART OF THE BRICKS IN SPACE PROJECT, DESIGNED TO INCREASE CHILDREN'S AWARENESS OF SPACE EXPLORATION.

LANDERS AND ROVERS

The first space probes to reach a planet or moon deliberately crash-landed on the surface, as they didn't have the technology to make a cushioned landing. Others have been accidentally damaged during descending or landing – the riskiest moments in a space probe's journey. But some have survived to send back vital information.

Smash!

The spectacular Deep Impact mission sent a space probe blasting into the nucleus of a comet called Tempel 1. The probe smashed into the comet at a speed of 37,000 km/h, creating a 150-m-wide crater and throwing up material from the comet's nucleus.

This image was taken 67 seconds after Deep Impact's space probe crashed into Tempel 1.

HOW DO PROBES LAND?

Once close to its target, gravity pulls a lander probe towards a planet or moon's surface. It will speed up unless some form of braking device is employed. Parachutes, jet thrusters or a skycrane all help the probe to land softly.

PIGGYBACK PROBES

Some lander probes, like Rosetta's Philae and the Huygens probe, hitch a ride on a bigger orbiter probe before being dropped to the surface. Huygens was released from the Cassini orbiter in 2005 to land on Saturn's moon, Titan – over 1.2 billion km from Earth.

Roving Around

The first successful rover – a space probe that can move about the surface of a planet or a moon – was the car-sized Lunakhod 1. It landed on the Moon in 1970 and was controlled remotely by scientists from the Soviet Union.

Three generations of Mars rovers: these are replicas, as the real rovers are still on Mars!

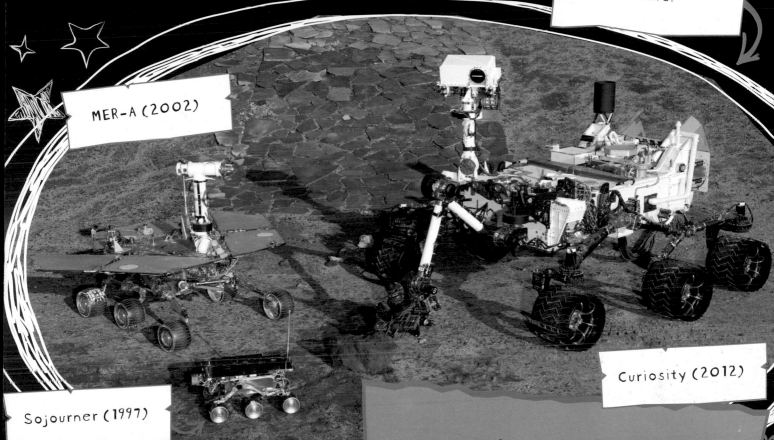

MER-A (2002)

Curiosity (2012)

Sojourner (1997)

MARS MOVERS

Viking 1 and 2 were the first lander probes on Mars. They have been followed by three generations of Mars rovers. The first, the 65-cm-long Sojourner, landed in 1997. It was followed in 2002 by the 1.65-m-long MER-A and MER-B rovers and the 3-m-long rover Curiosity in 2012.

36,700
THE NUMBER OF PHOTOS THAT CURIOSITY TOOK DURING ITS FIRST YEAR ON MARS. TO CELEBRATE ONE YEAR ON THE PLANET, IT EVEN PLAYED 'HAPPY BIRTHDAY' TO ITSELF – THE FIRST KNOWN MUSIC ON MARS!

SPACE MEN AND WOMEN

With a cry of, 'Poyekhali!' ('Off we go!'), Yuri Gagarin blasted off in his 2.3-metre-wide Vostok 1 spacecraft in 1961 to become the first person in space. More than 500 astronauts have followed Gagarin, including 26-year-old Valentina Tereshkova, the first woman in space, in 1963.

Men On The Moon

Twelve amazing astronauts have set foot on the Moon as part of the Apollo missions (1969–72). The Apollo missions were complex, yet they were achieved using an on-board computer with just 64 kilobytes of memory – half a million times less memory than a modern smartphone!

Neil Armstrong took this photo of his fellow astronaut Buzz Aldrin during the Apollo 11 moon landing in 1969.

20–30

THE NUMBER OF SECONDS' WORTH OF FUEL LEFT IN APOLLO 11'S TANKS AS IT LANDED ON THE LUNAR SURFACE, CARRYING THE FIRST ASTRONAUTS TO SET FOOT ON THE MOON – NEIL ARMSTRONG AND EDWIN 'BUZZ' ALDRIN.

SPACE TOURISTS

A handful of people who were not fully trained astronauts have paid large sums to travel into space. The first, Dennis Tito, spent almost eight days on board the International Space Station in 2001. A number of companies are developing their own private spacecraft to give people a taste of space in the future.

Suited and Booted

A spacesuit is a mini survival capsule, protecting an astronaut from the extremes of heat, cold and harmful radiation in space. NASA's EMU suit is made up of 13 layers and would weigh 127 kg on Earth. It can take up to an hour to put on and features liquid-cooled underwear, a backpack that recycles air for the astronaut to breathe and gloves with heated fingertips.

SPACEWALKS

Extra-vehicular Activity (EVA), or spacewalks, are where astronauts leave the safety of their spacecraft and venture out into space. Nearly all spacewalkers remain attached to the spacecraft by a tether, which supplies oxygen and electrical power to their EVA spacesuit.

Bruce McCandless enjoys a wild EVA using a Manned Maneuvring Unit (MMU). This jetpack fires nitrogen gas through 24 jet nozzles to change direction in space

WHEN WAS THE FIRST EVA?

The first EVA was performed by Alexei Leonov in 1965. It lasted 12 minutes.

NASA Nappy

Spacewalking astronauts wear a Maximum Absorbency Garment while in space. This is a high-tech adult nappy that can absorb up to 2 litres of fluids.

ASTRONAUT TRAINING

There's a vast amount of training to be done before an astronaut can strap in for lift-off. Astronauts need to be physically fit and mentally sharp.

Know Your Way Around

Every astronaut has to be familiar with the controls and procedures in their spacecraft. This training can last months, or even years, and takes place in realistic models of the spacecraft. Every element, from how to put on a spacesuit to what to do in an emergency situation, must be learned and practised.

DEALING WITH MICROGRAVITY

In space, astronauts have to deal with microgravity, which means that they, and any loose objects in space, experience weightlessness and float around. This can have disorientating effects on the body, so trainee astronauts get to experience it beforehand in aircraft nicknamed 'vomit comets'. These fly up and down sharply to create 20–30-second periods of weightlessness.

astronauts training in a 'vomit comet'

Going Swimmingly

NASA astronauts get to train in the world's largest indoor swimming pool. The Neutral Buoyancy Lab is 61.6 m by 31.1 m and 12.2 m deep. The tank holds full-size models of spacecraft and allows astronauts to simulate some of the movements needed to perform a spacewalk.

803

THE NUMBER OF DAYS SPENT IN SPACE BY RUSSIA'S SERGEI KRIKALEV, WHO HAS LIVED ON BOARD FOUR DIFFERENT CRAFT: SOYUZ, SPACE SHUTTLE AND THE MIR AND ISS SPACE STATIONS.

MISSION SPECIALISTS

Most astronauts are either talented scientists or jet pilots. Each has their own special tasks to perform during the mission, such as running experiments inside the spacecraft or operating a giant robot arm to move equipment in space. Many astronauts are cross-trained so they can also perform other crew members' tasks.

underwater training at the Neutral Buoyancy Lab

THE INTERNATIONAL SPACE STATION

Look up! Over 400 km above Earth, orbiting the planet once every 90 minutes, is the biggest ever piece of space hardware – the International Space Station (ISS). Built by a partnership of 16 countries, the ISS is 74 m long and 110 m wide, a little bigger than a football pitch.

Piece-By-Piece

The ISS was flown into space, piece by piece, starting in 1998. Gradually, new modules and parts have been added to its central spine, including eight pairs of giant solar-array wings (SAWs). Each SAW contains 32,800 solar cells that convert energy from the Sun into electricity to power the ISS.

ONE BIG BUILDING SITE

The ISS was space's biggest building site, requiring giant robot arms, many space flights and over 1,100 hours of spacewalks by 113 different astronauts to complete. The longest single EVA was by Susan J. Helms and James S. Voss in 2001, and lasted 8 hours and 56 minutes.

This is a view of the ISS from the Space Shuttle Atlantis.

Roomy

ISS crews work and relax in modules, which provide as much living space as a six-bedroom house. The ISS includes a gym, two bathrooms and docking points for the spacecraft that ferry crew, supplies and parts to and from the ISS. The crew can admire the view from the cupola, a 360° window, or even surf the web and post on social media from space!

ISS crews are made up of six or seven people, seen here enjoying a zero-gravity meal!

The ISS weighs 420,000 kg, equal to more than 300 cars on Earth.

While on an EVA, working on the outside of the ISS in 2008, astronaut Heide Stefanyshyn-Piper lost grip of her high-tech tool bag, which floated away. The bag, which contained around US$100,000 of equipment, burned up in Earth's atmosphere a year later.

SERIOUS SCIENCE

It's not all fun on board the ISS. As a semi-permanent base in space, the space station allows astronauts to investigate both Earth and space, and perform hundreds of science experiments on space's long-term effects on people, plants and materials.

144
THE NUMBER OF SPACECRAFT FLIGHTS TO THE INTERNATIONAL SPACE STATION BETWEEN 1998 AND 2014.

LIFE IN SPACE

Some of the science experiments on board manned spacecraft have focused on the astronauts themselves. They have taught us about space's effect on the human body and helped us to understand how to equip astronauts for long missions away from Earth.

Space Side Effects

Astronauts can be disorientated and feel sick in their first few days in space. The lack of gravity makes blood rise up their bodies, from the legs into the chest and head. This gives astronauts a puffy face and sometimes leads to sinus pain and congestion.

KEEPING FIT

Without the gravity found on Earth, an astronaut's muscles grow weaker, as they are not required to support the body. The ISS is equipped with a weights machine, as well as a treadmill and exercise bike, to help maintain muscle strength on a long mission. The crew exercises for 2-3 hours each day.

Russian astronaut Maxim Suraev exercises on the treadmill on the ISS.

5

THE TYPICAL AMOUNT IN CENTIMETRES THAT AN ASTRONAUT GROWS TALLER IN SPACE, DUE TO THE LACK OF GRAVITY PUSHING DOWN ON THEIR SPINE.

Food For Thought

Early astronaut food was dry cubes or purees, squeezed out of toothpaste-like tubes. Today, many foods are dried and sealed in pouches to save weight, and have to be rehydrated and heated on board. Food is eaten off a dinner tray equipped with straps, so that it can be fixed to a wall or table to stop it floating away.

A meal on board the ISS. The utensils are attached to the tray with magnets to stop them floating away!

HOW DO YOU 'GO' IN SPACE?

Very carefully! Space toilets use flowing air, rather than water, to flush away the waste liquid and solids. On the ISS, the liquid waste is filtered and cleaned and then used again as drinking water. The solid waste is kept in bags in a storage container until the spacecraft returns to Earth.

CLEANING UP

In the microgravity of space, water doesn't run downwards like it does on Earth. It floats in all directions and can damage on-board computers. To help astronauts keep clean, scientists have developed toothpaste and shampoo that do not need to be rinsed out. On the ISS, astronauts take sponge baths, using damp cloths to clean themselves.

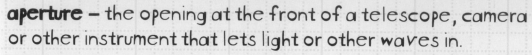

GLOSSARY

aperture – the opening at the front of a telescope, camera or other instrument that lets light or other waves in.

atmosphere – the blanket of gases that surrounds the surface of a planet.

black hole – an object in space with such strong gravity that nothing nearby can escape its pull, including light.

concave – having a curved, inwards shape – like a bowl.

exoplanet – a planet found outside of the solar system.

gravity – the invisible force of attraction between objects.

light year – the distance travelled by light in a year (approximately 9.4 trillion km).

matter – physical things that exist in space as solids, liquids or gases.

microgravity – the very weak pull of gravity, as experienced by astronauts in space, that makes them feel weightless.

orbit – to travel round another object in space, usually in an elliptical path.

payload – the cargo carried by a rocket or another launch vehicle from Earth into space.

radiation – energy, such as infrared, X-rays and visible light, that travels through space in waves.

reflector – a telescope that uses mirrors to reflect and focus light.

refractor – a telescope that uses lenses to focus light.

space probe – a machine sent into space to explore and send back information.

space station – a spacecraft designed to house humans in space, often for long periods of time.

thrust – the power used to push something forward.

FURTHER INFORMATION

Books

World in Infographics: Space
by Jon Richards and Ed Simkins (Wayland, 2013)

Space Travel Guides: Space Exploration
by Giles Sparrow (Franklin Watts, 2013)

Scientists Who Made History: Galileo Galilei
by Dr Mike Goldsmith (Wayland, 2014)

Websites

http://amazing-space.stsci.edu/resources/explorations/groundup/
A visual history of telescopes and how they have developed.

http://coolcosmos.ipac.caltech.edu/
A guide and gallery of infrared objects in space.

http://www.nasa.gov/mission_pages/station/main/#.VDZmZfldXHk
NASA's detailed web pages on the International Space Station.

INDEX